This Book Belongs to

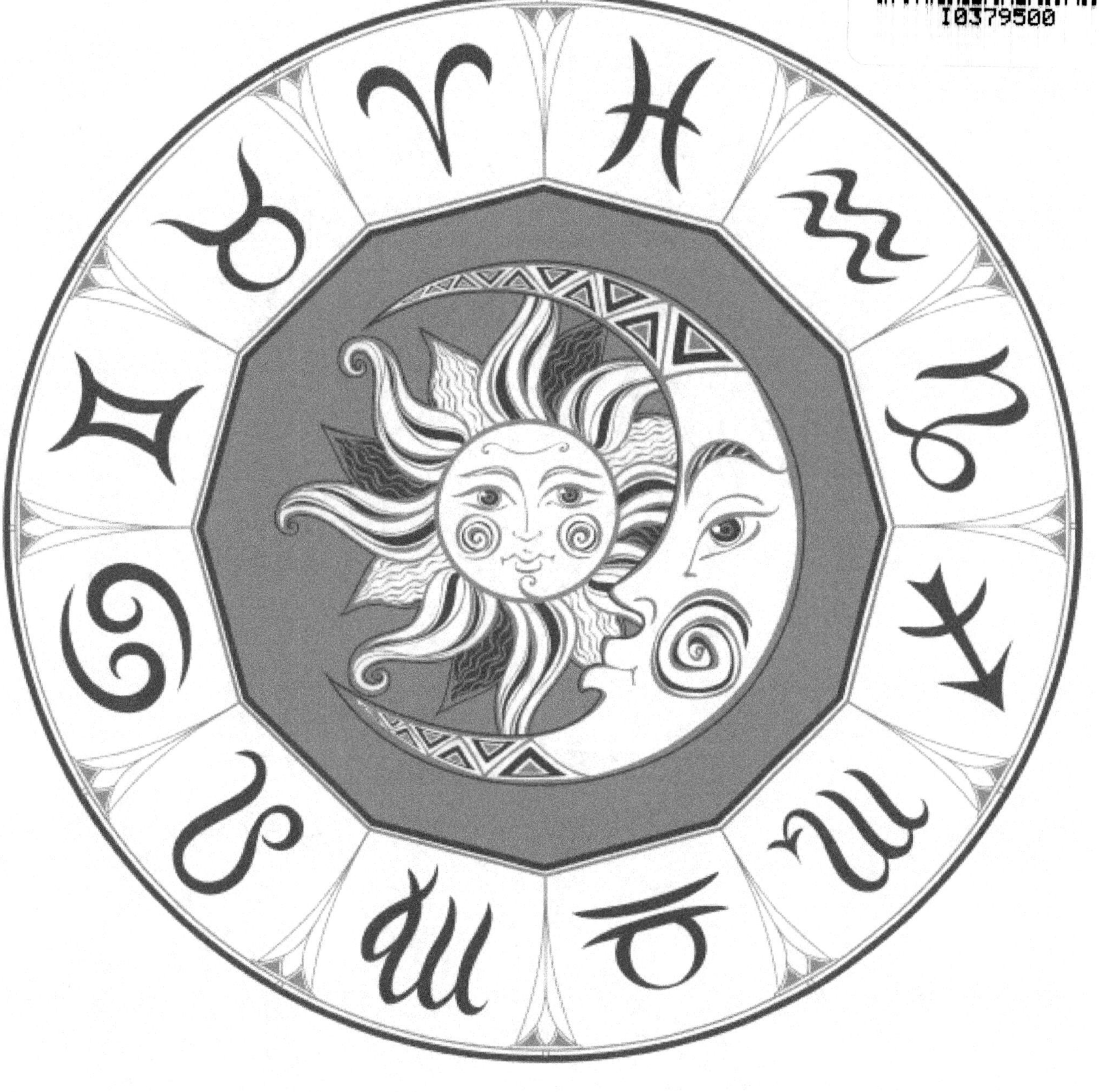

_____

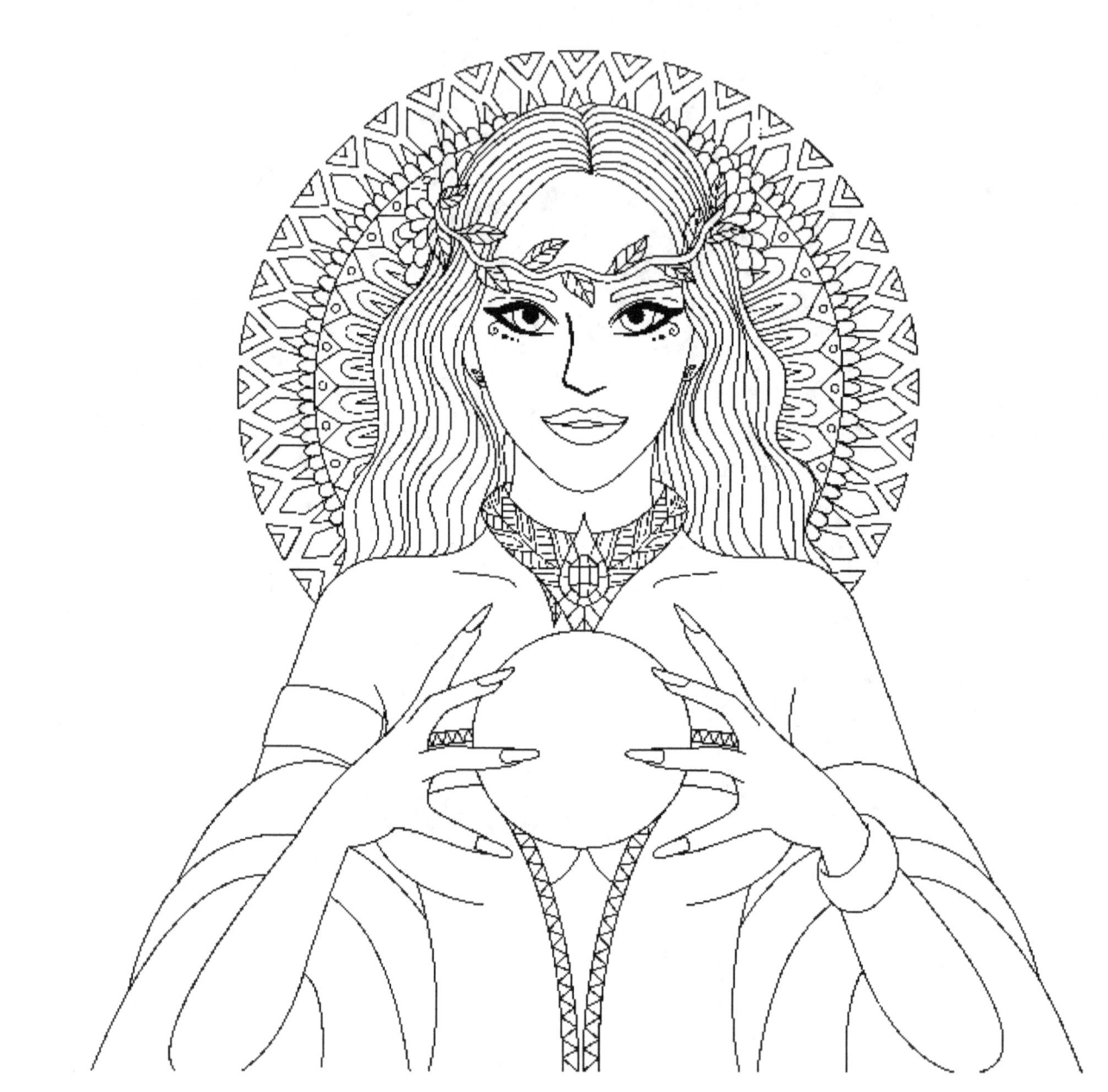

ZODIAC
ADULT COLORING BOOK

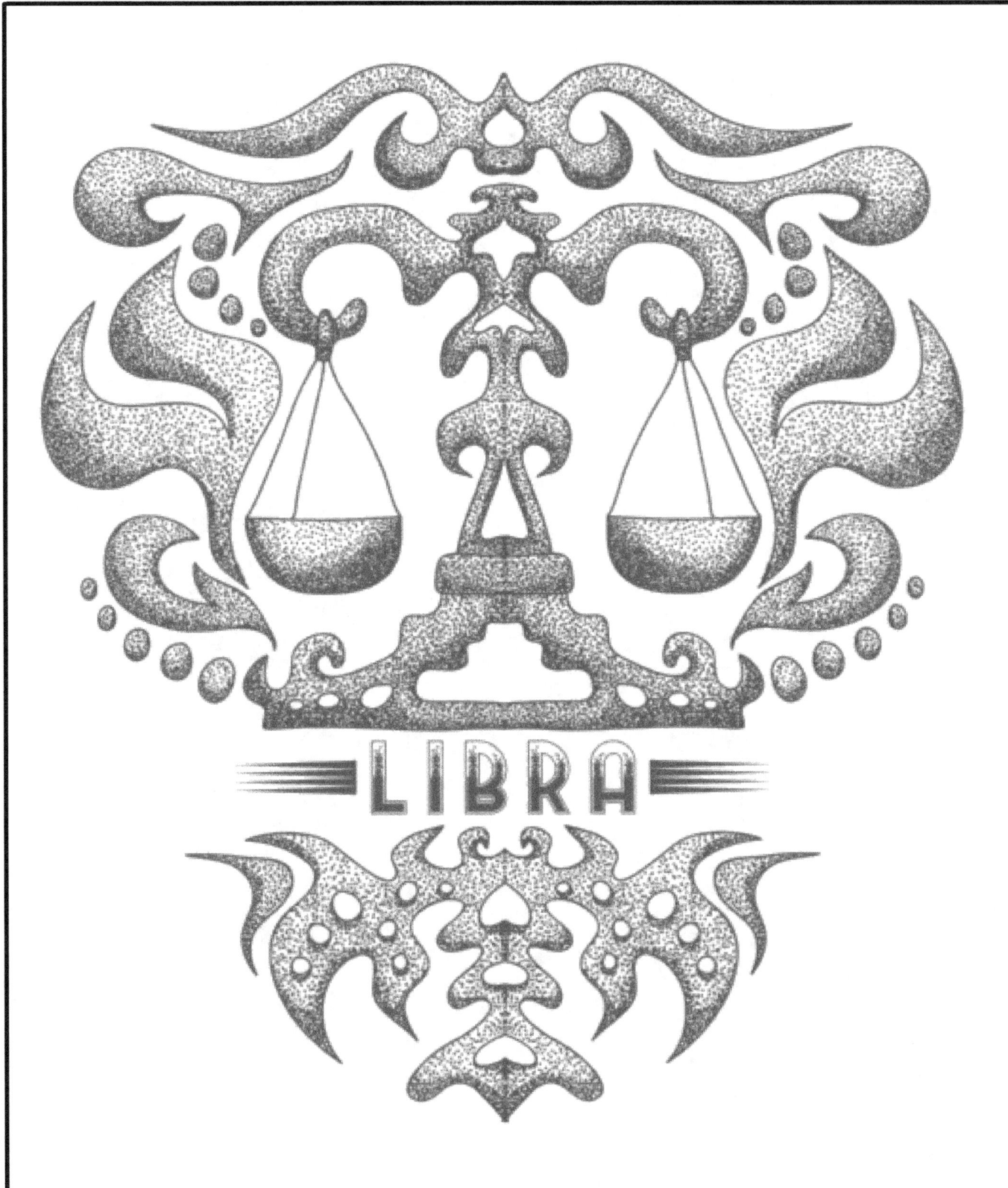

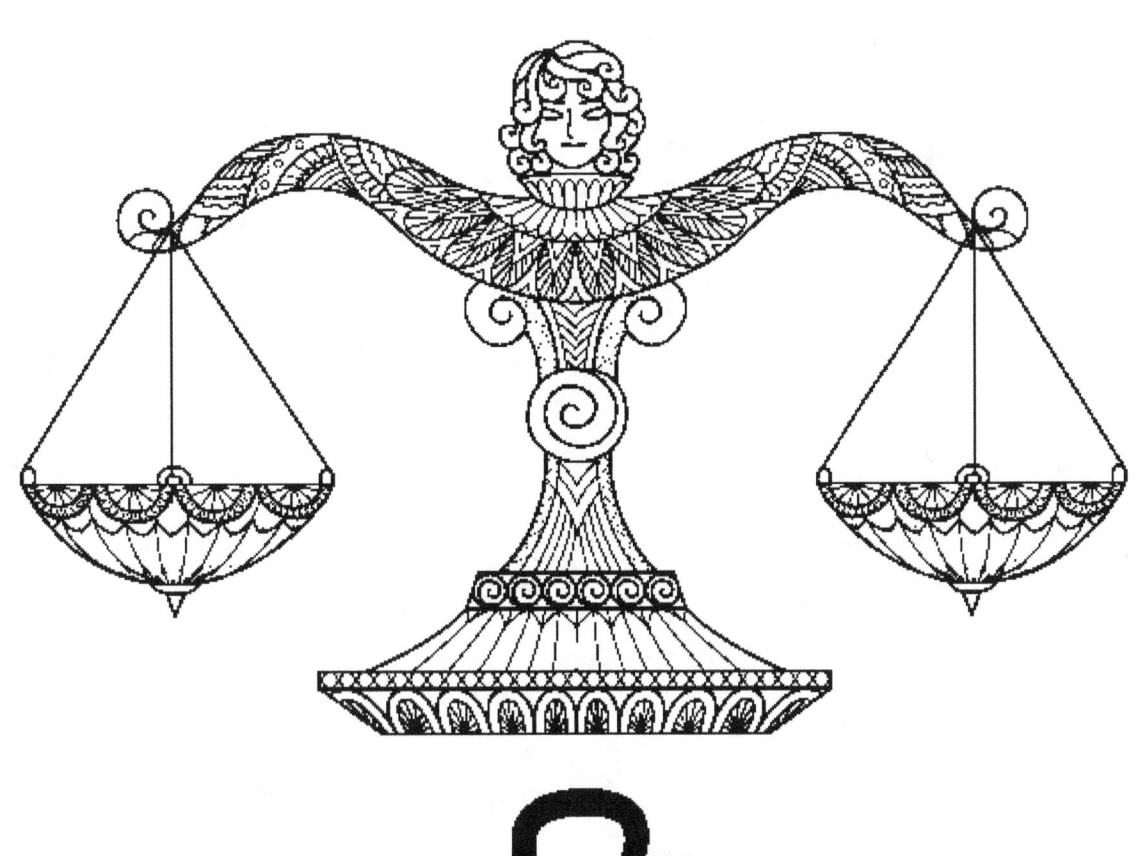

LIBRA

September 23 - October 22

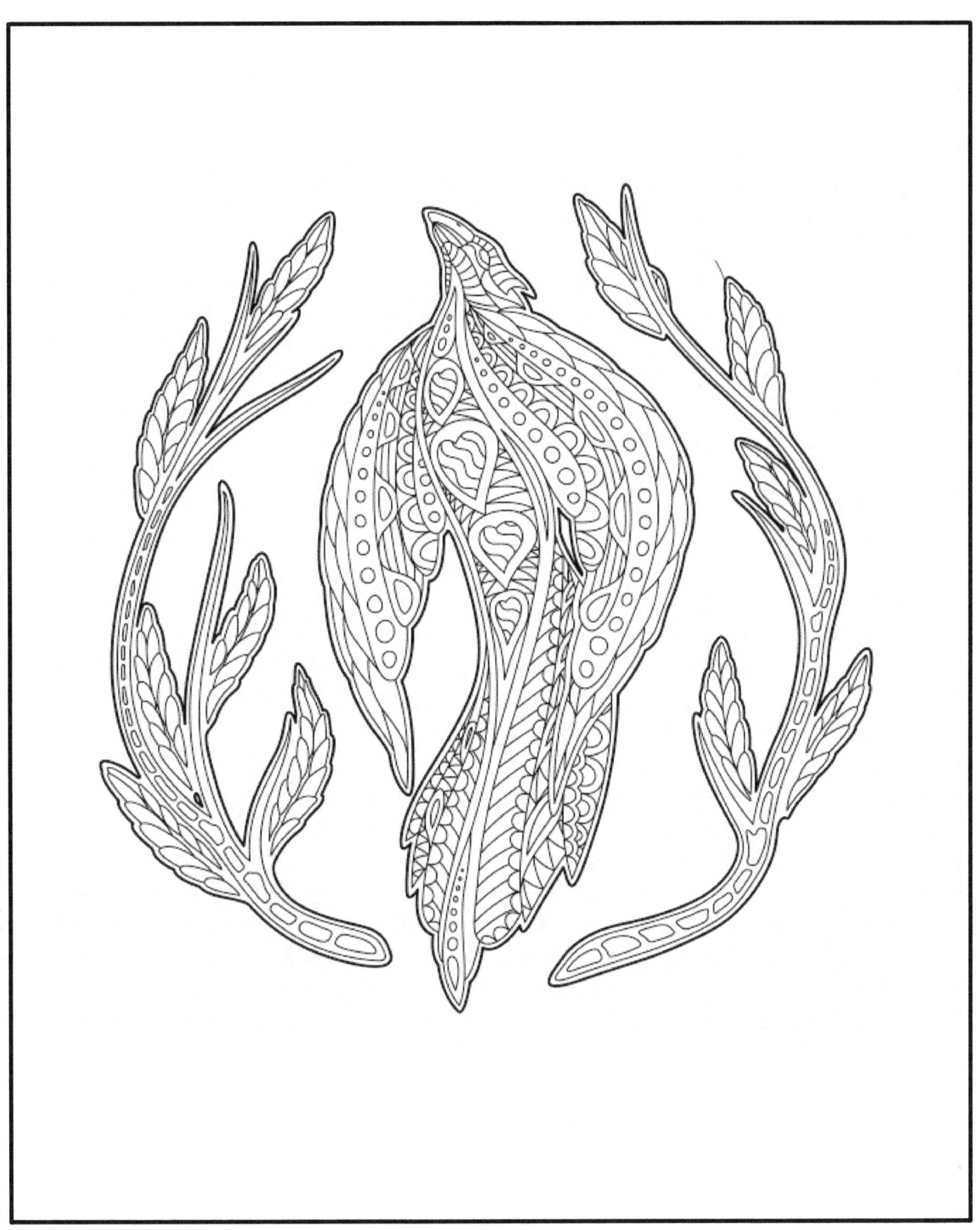

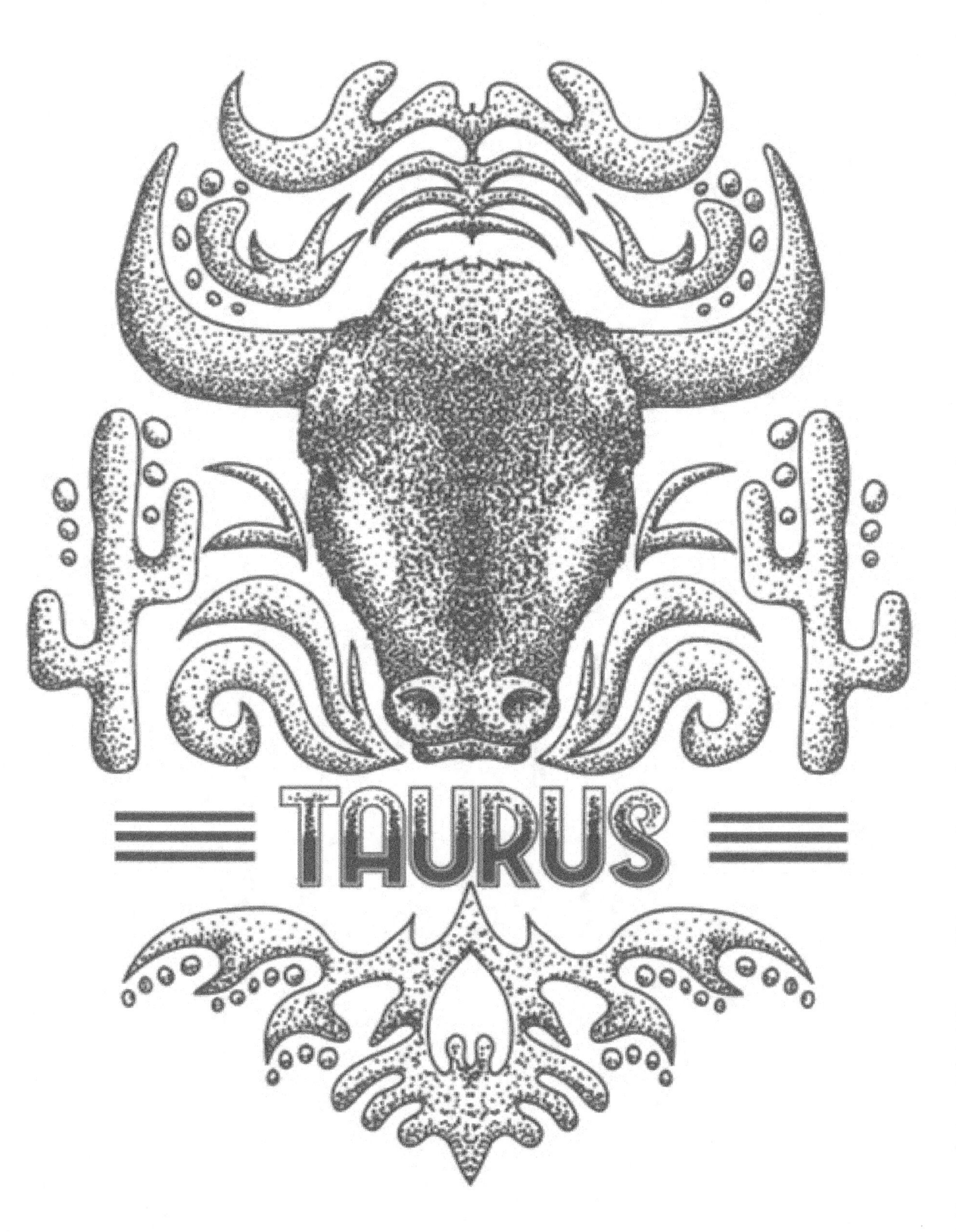

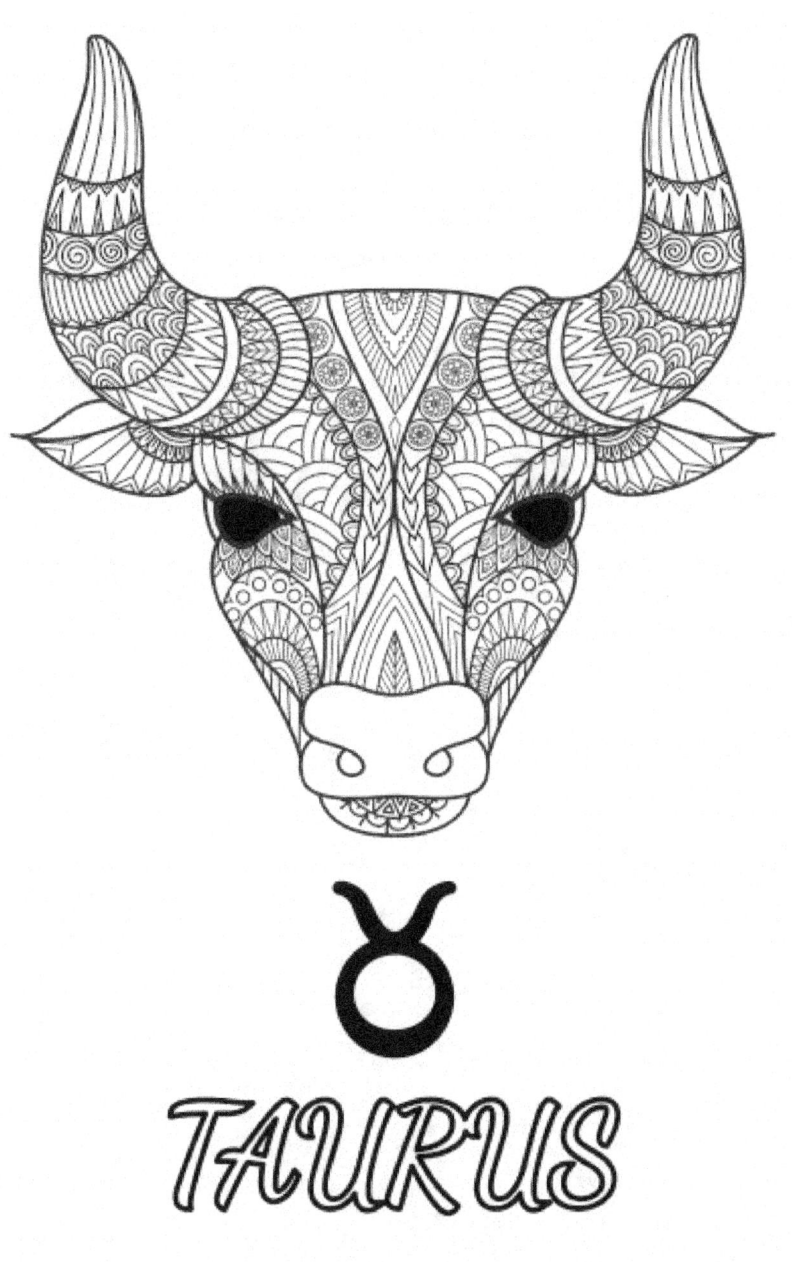

TAURUS

April 20 - May 20

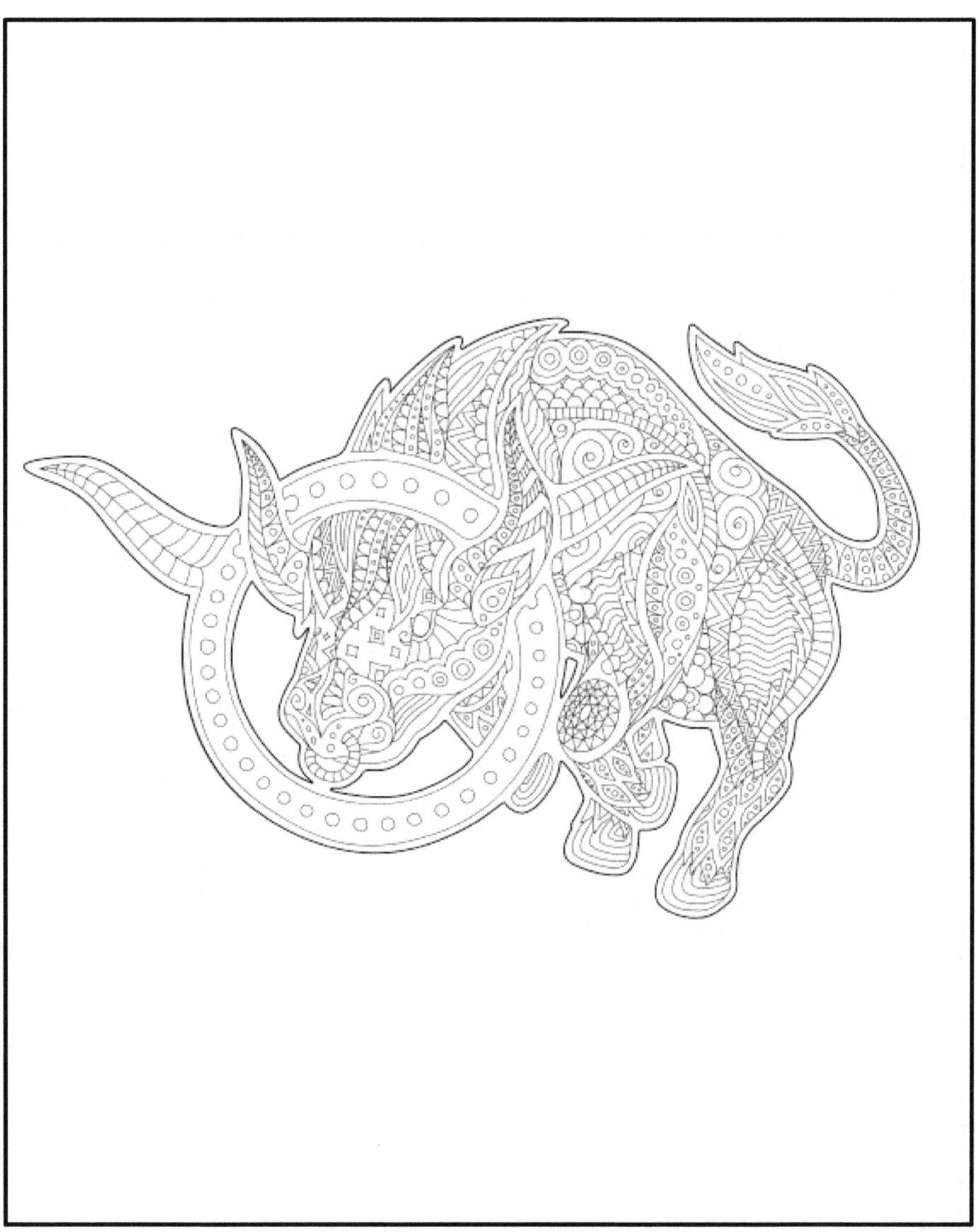

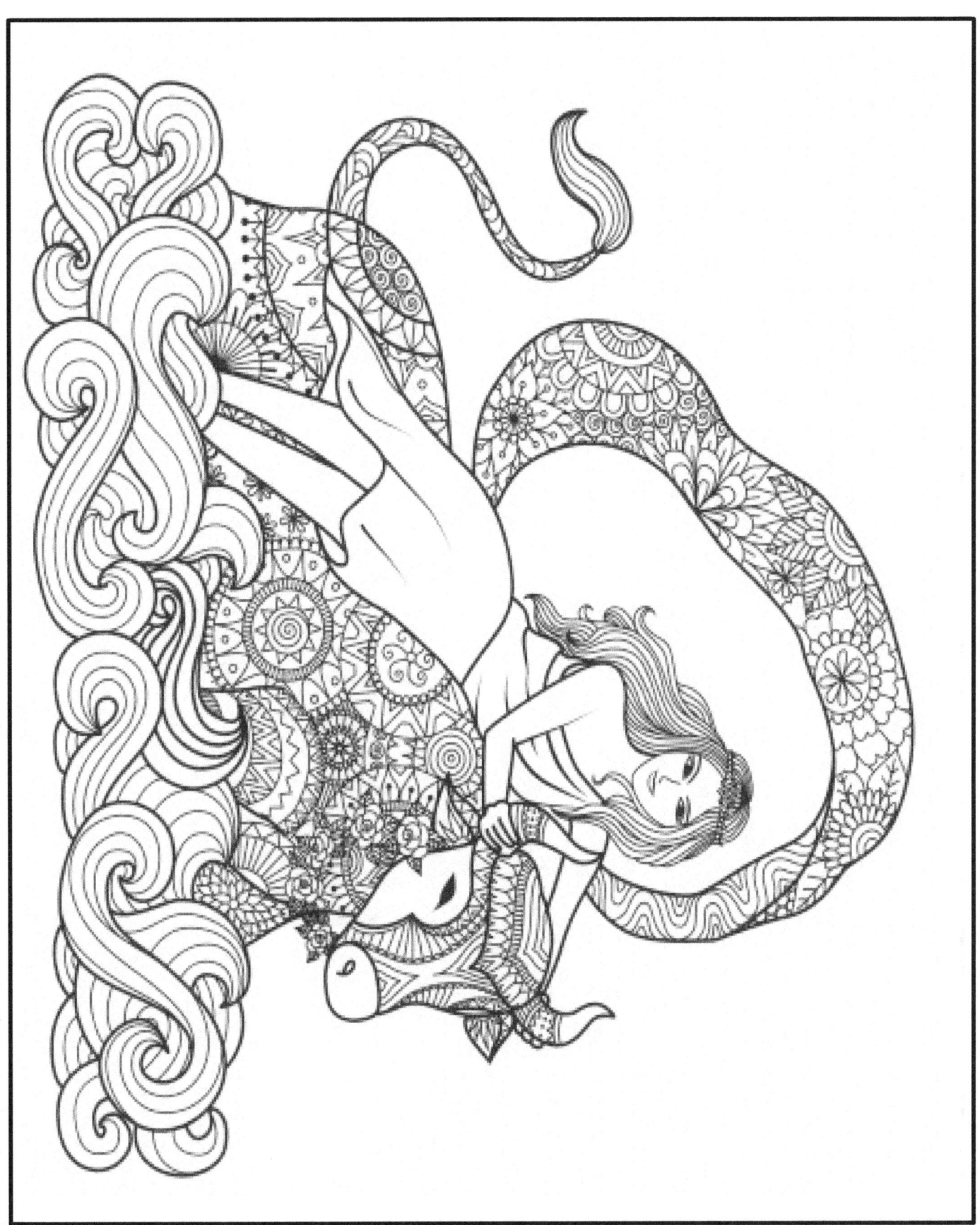

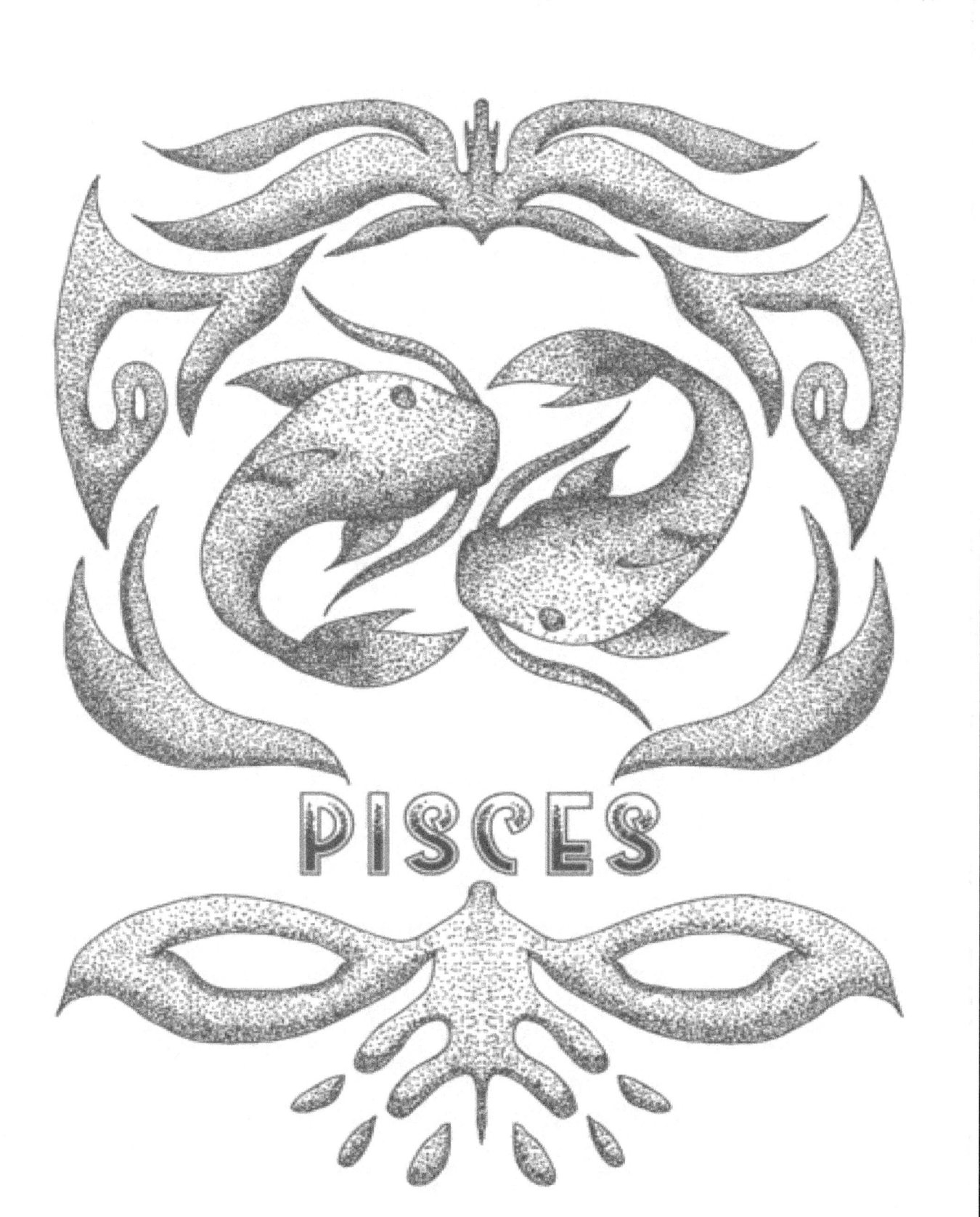

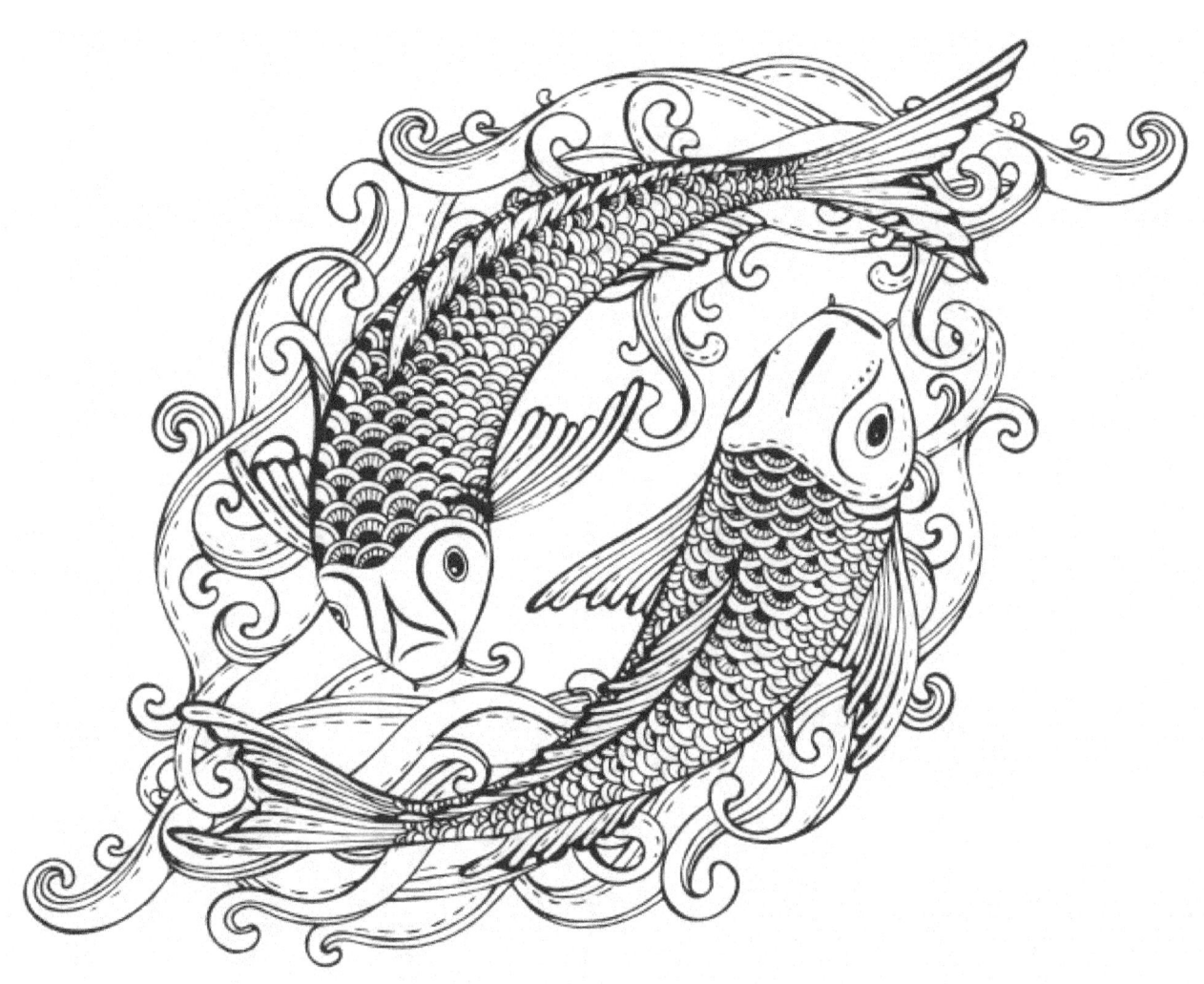

PISCES

February 19 - March 20

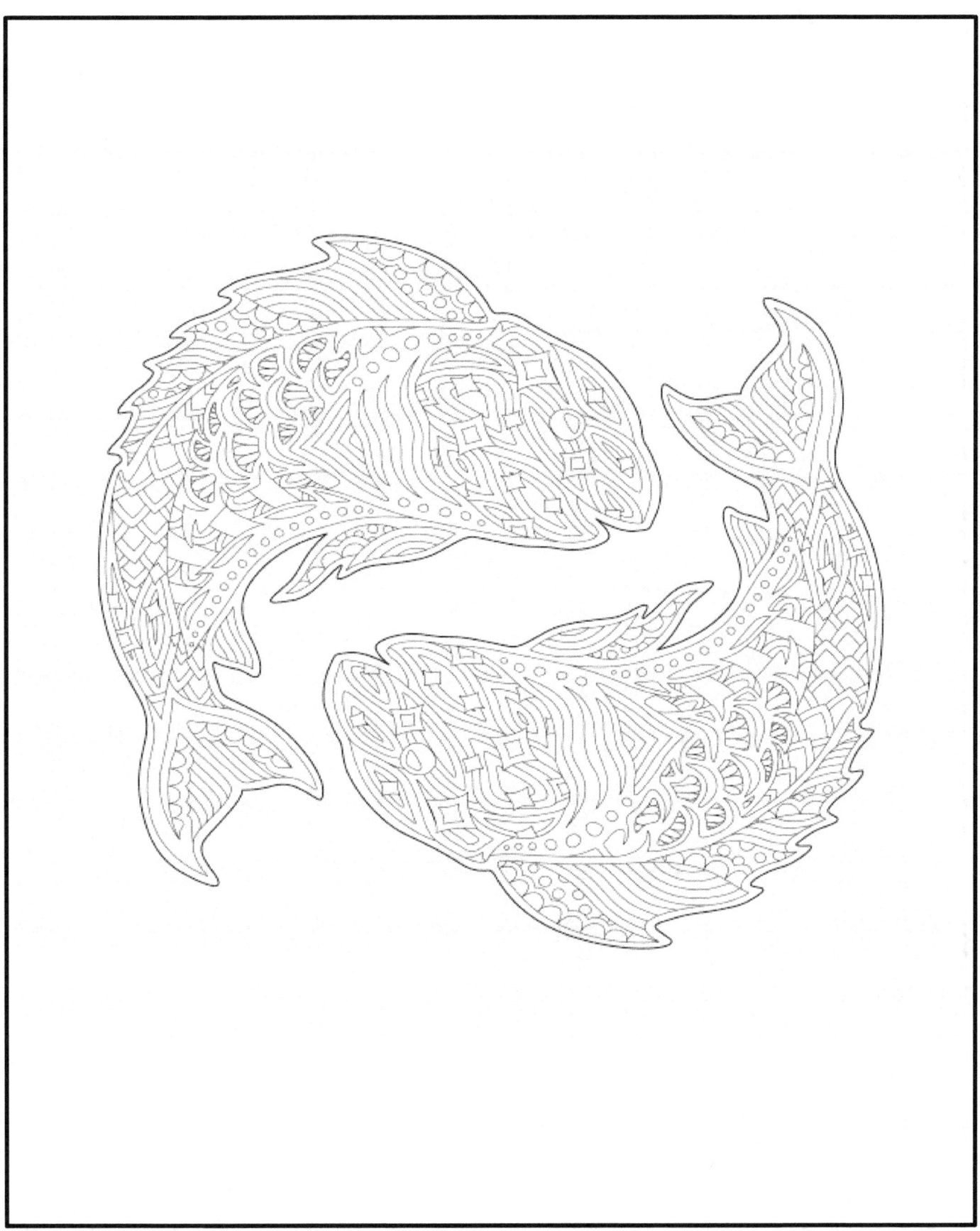

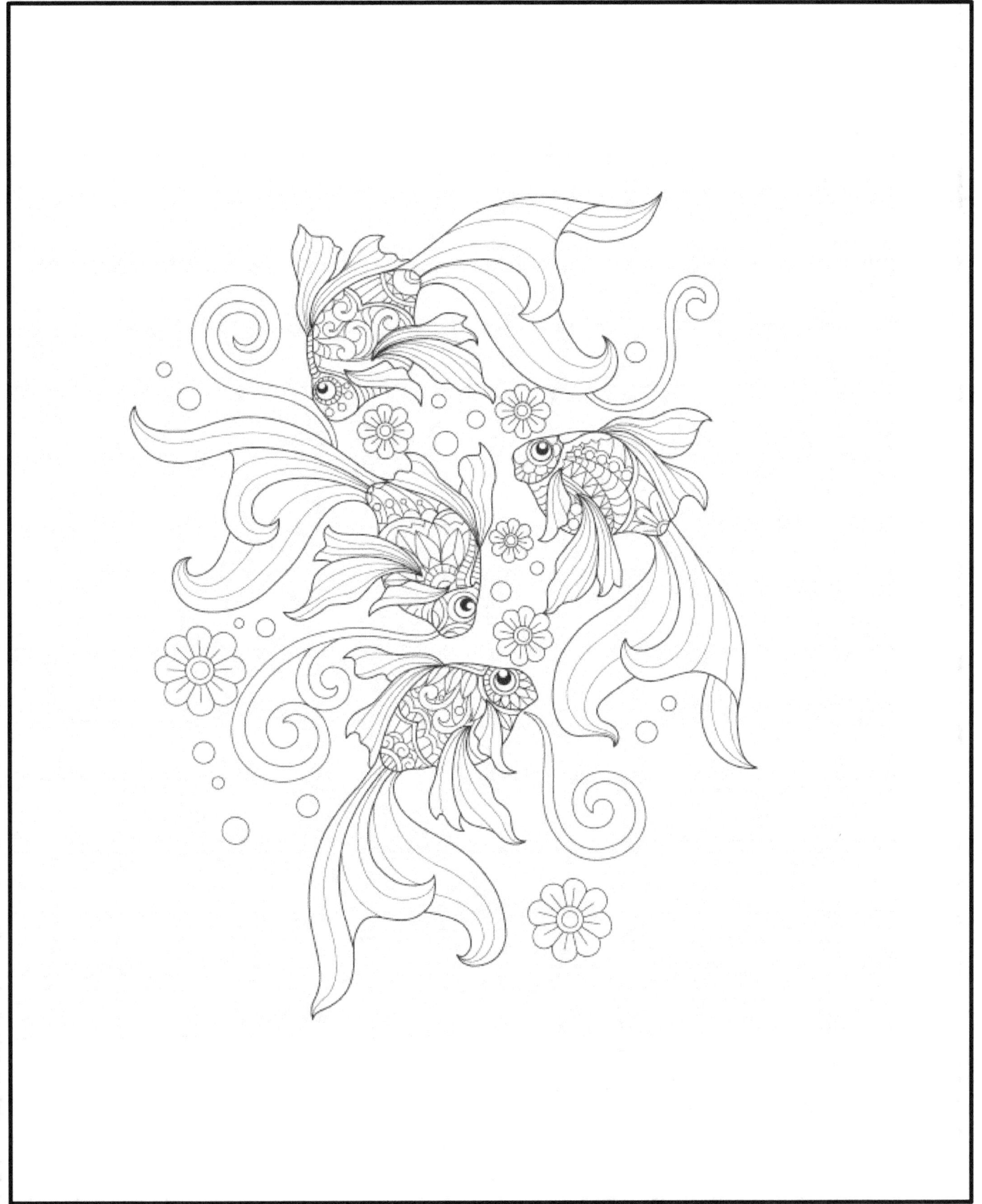

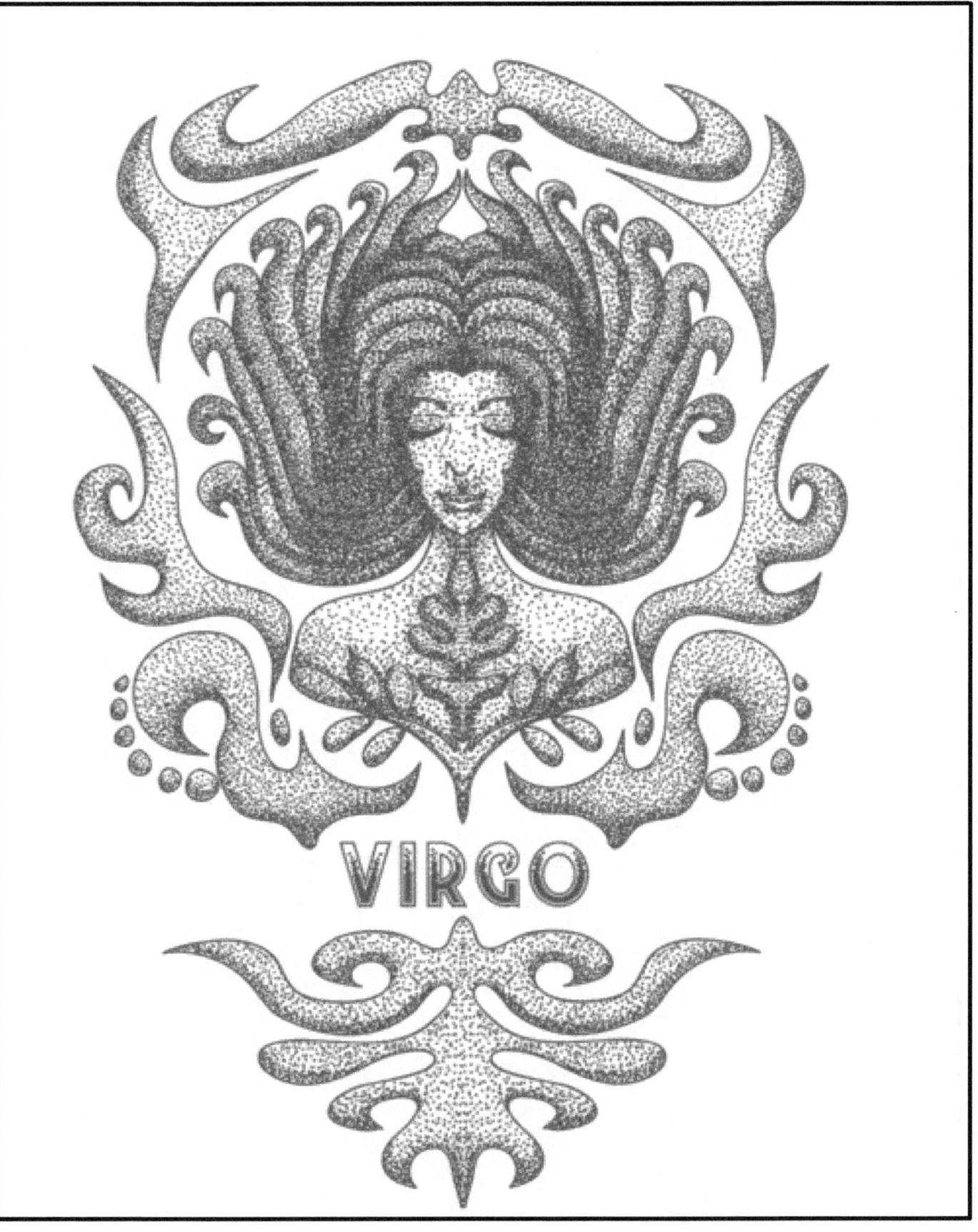

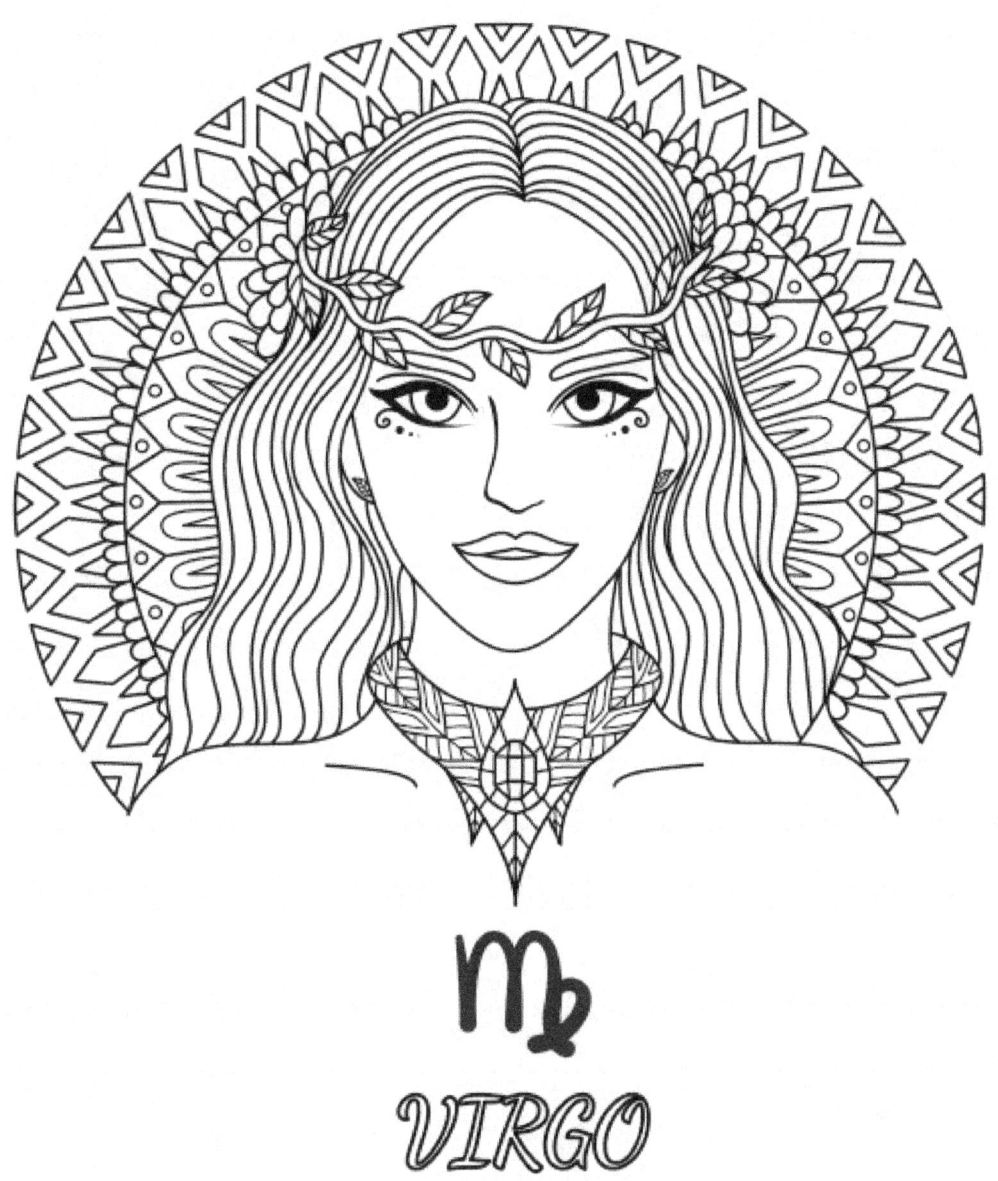

VIRGO

August 23 - September 22

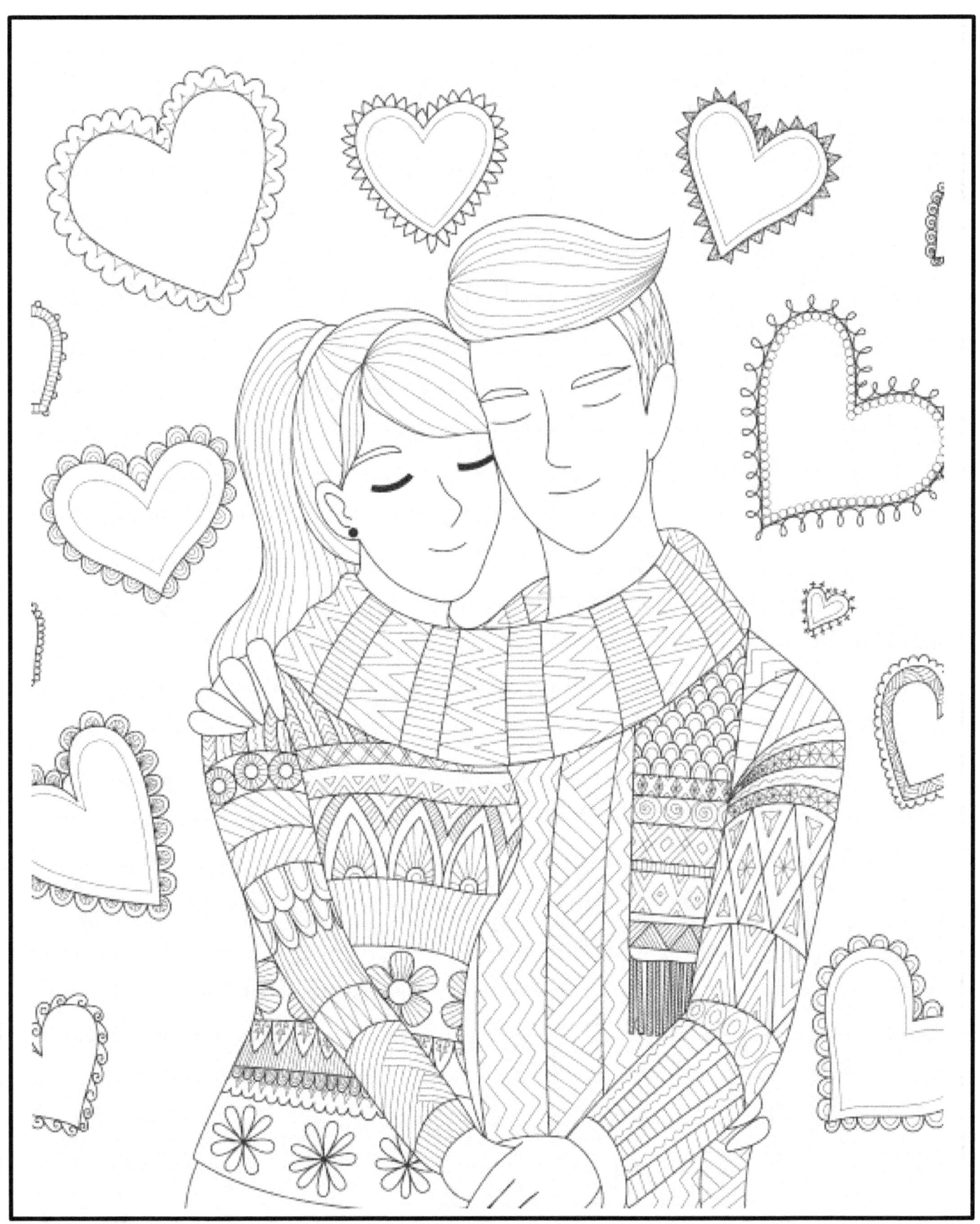

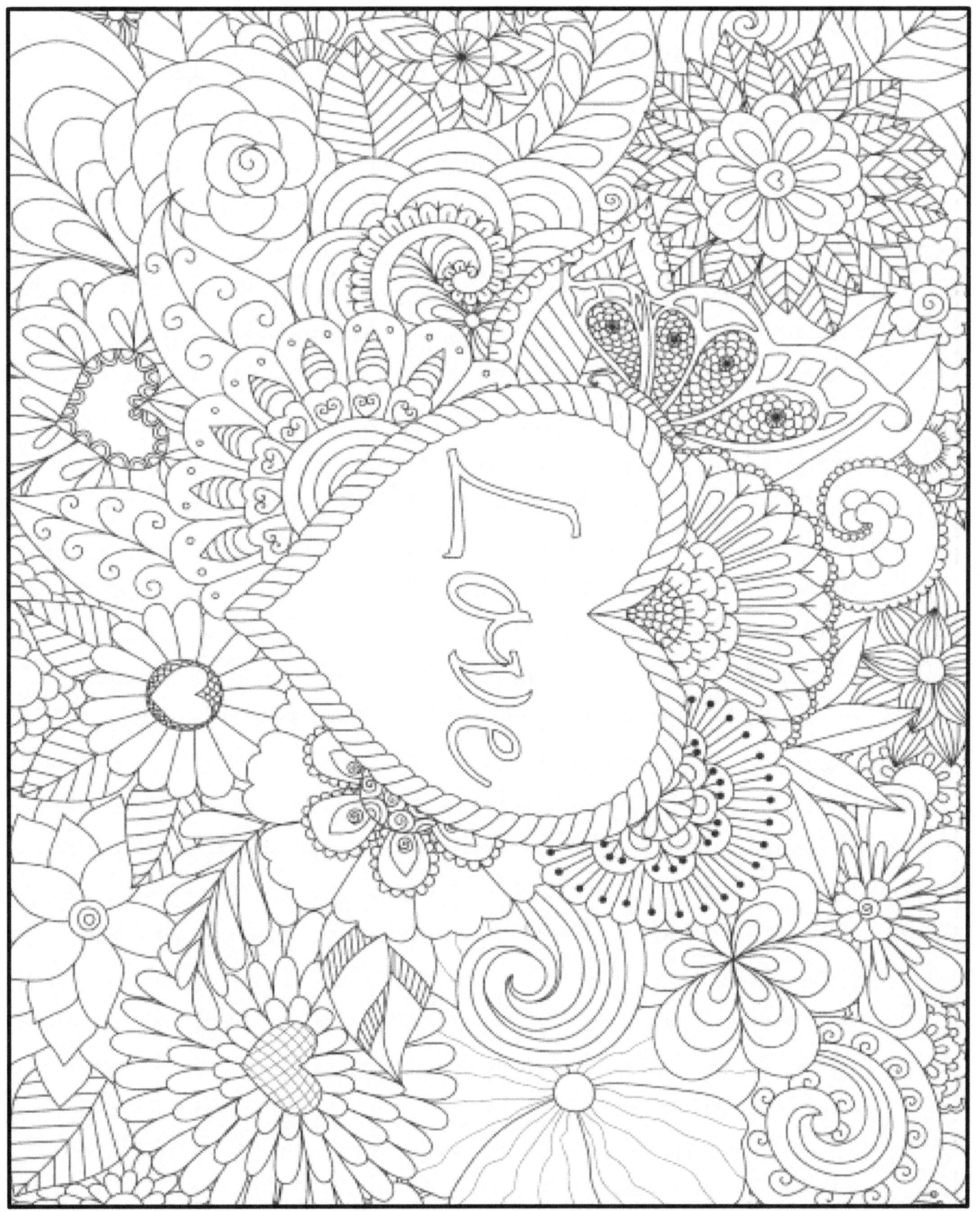

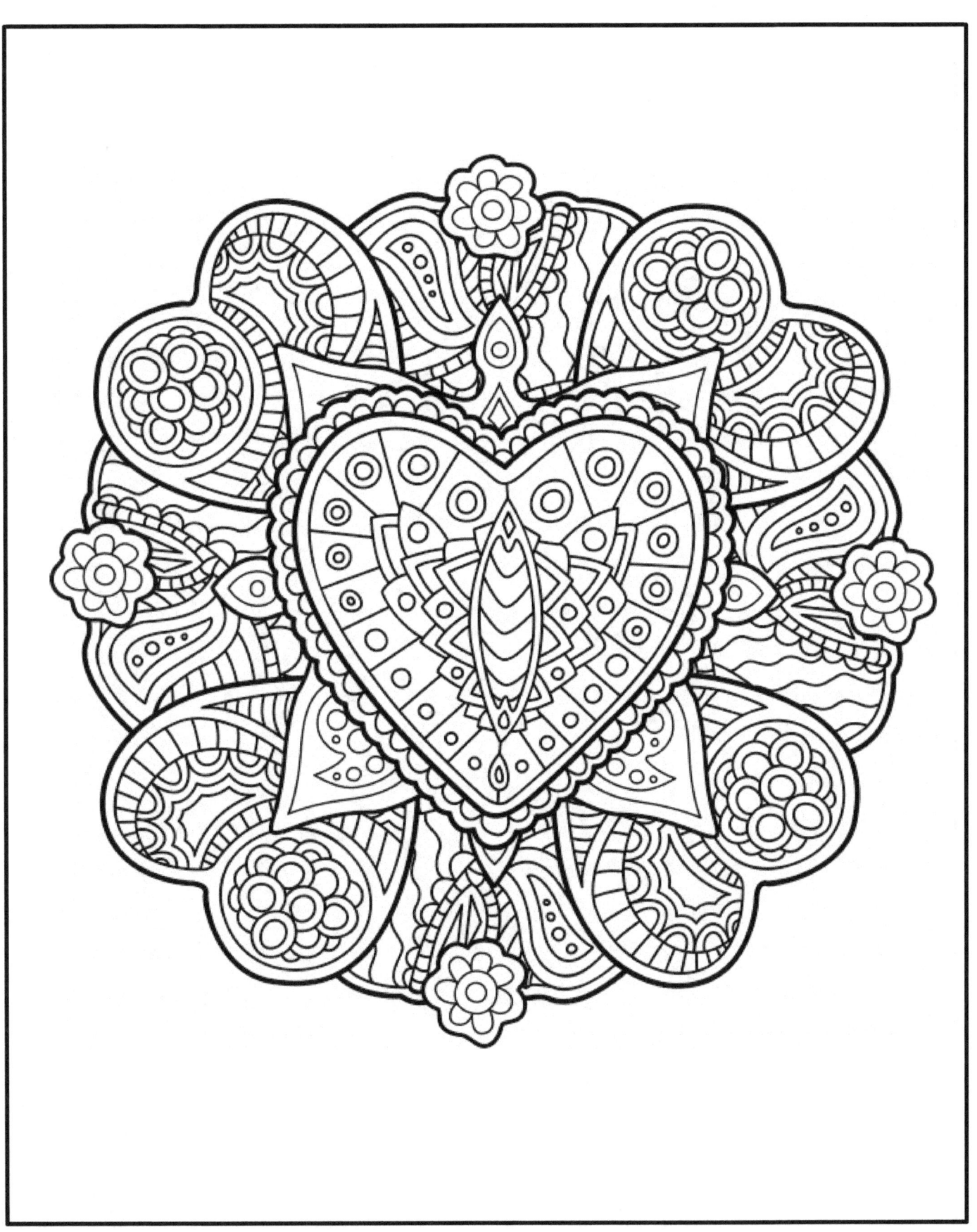

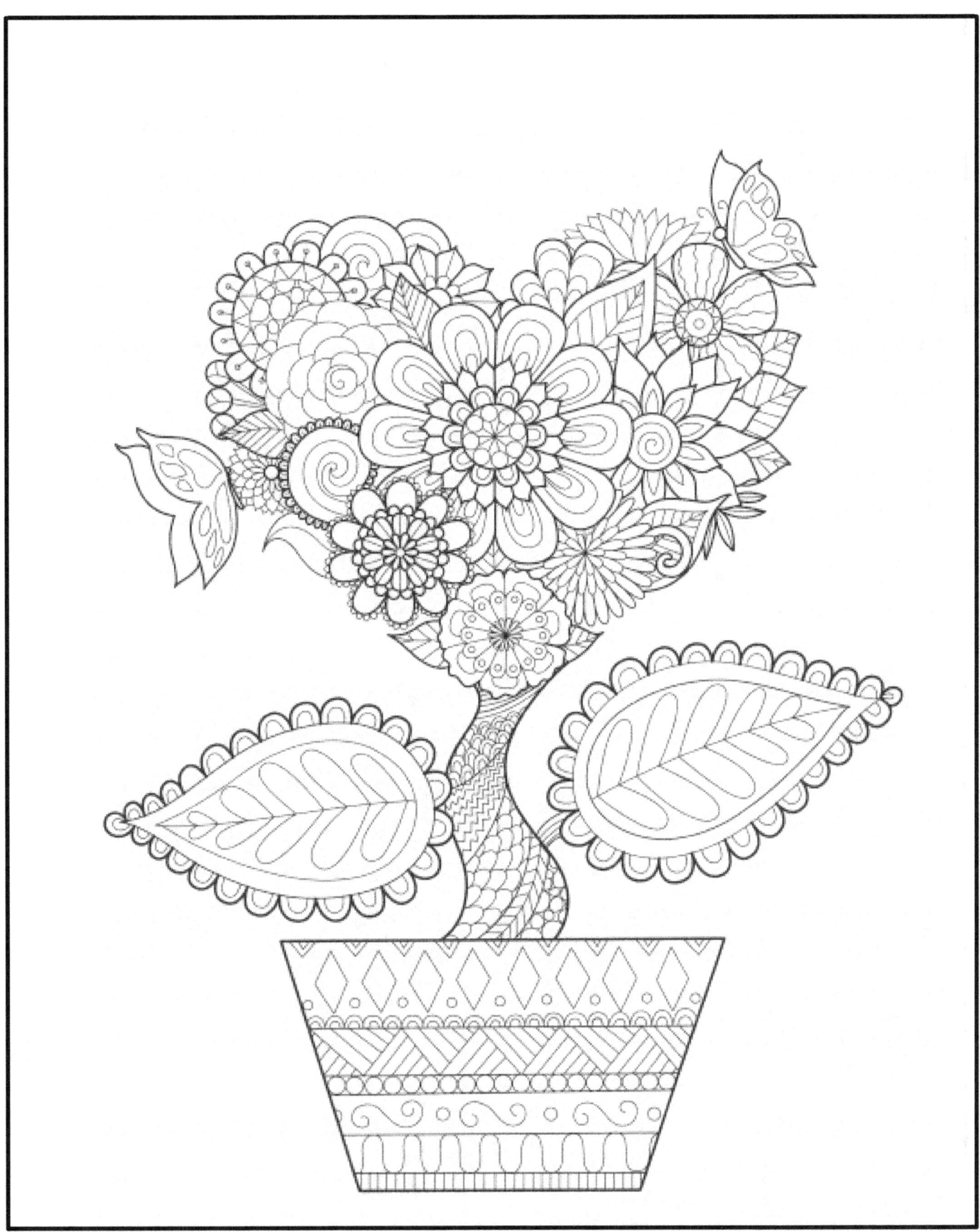

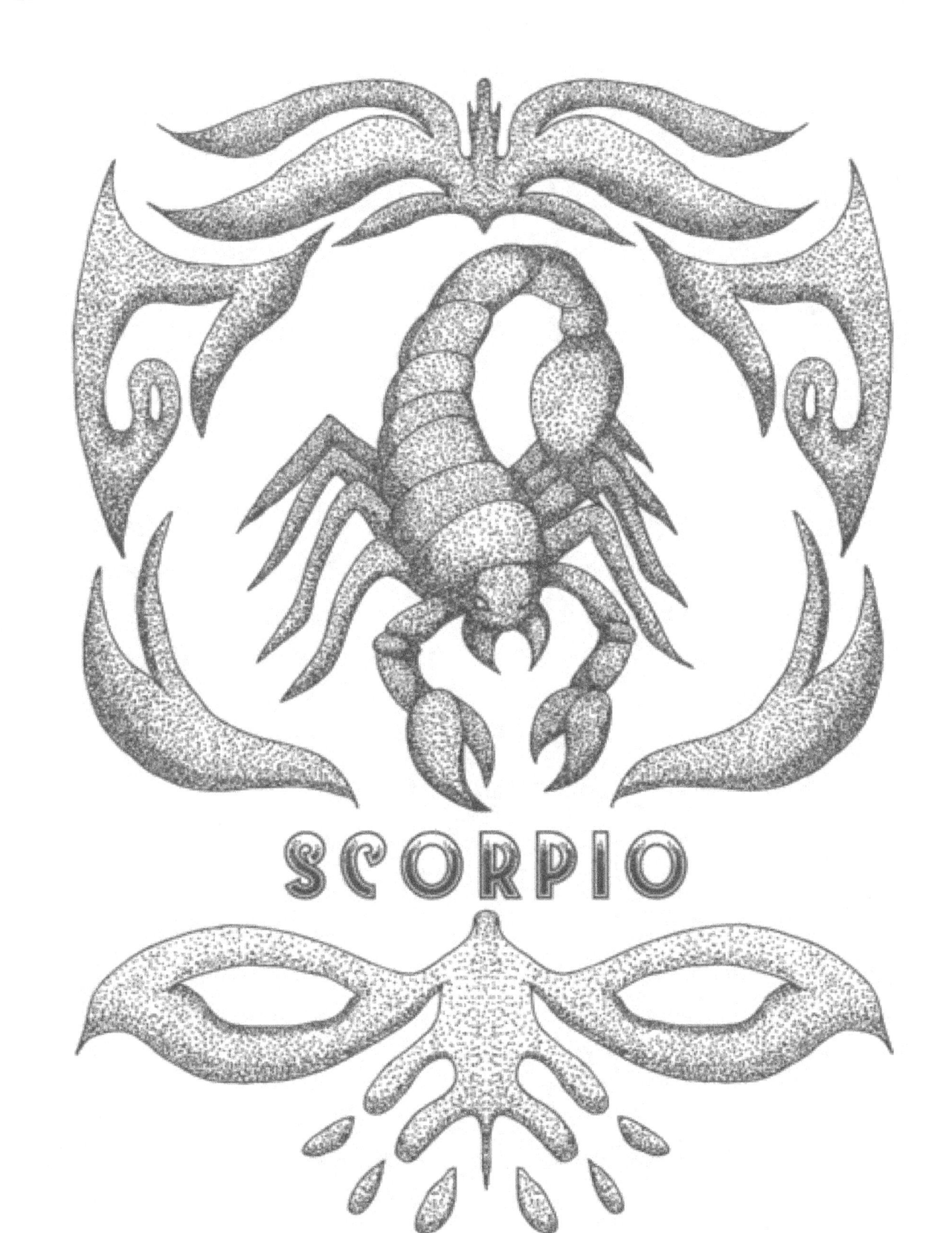

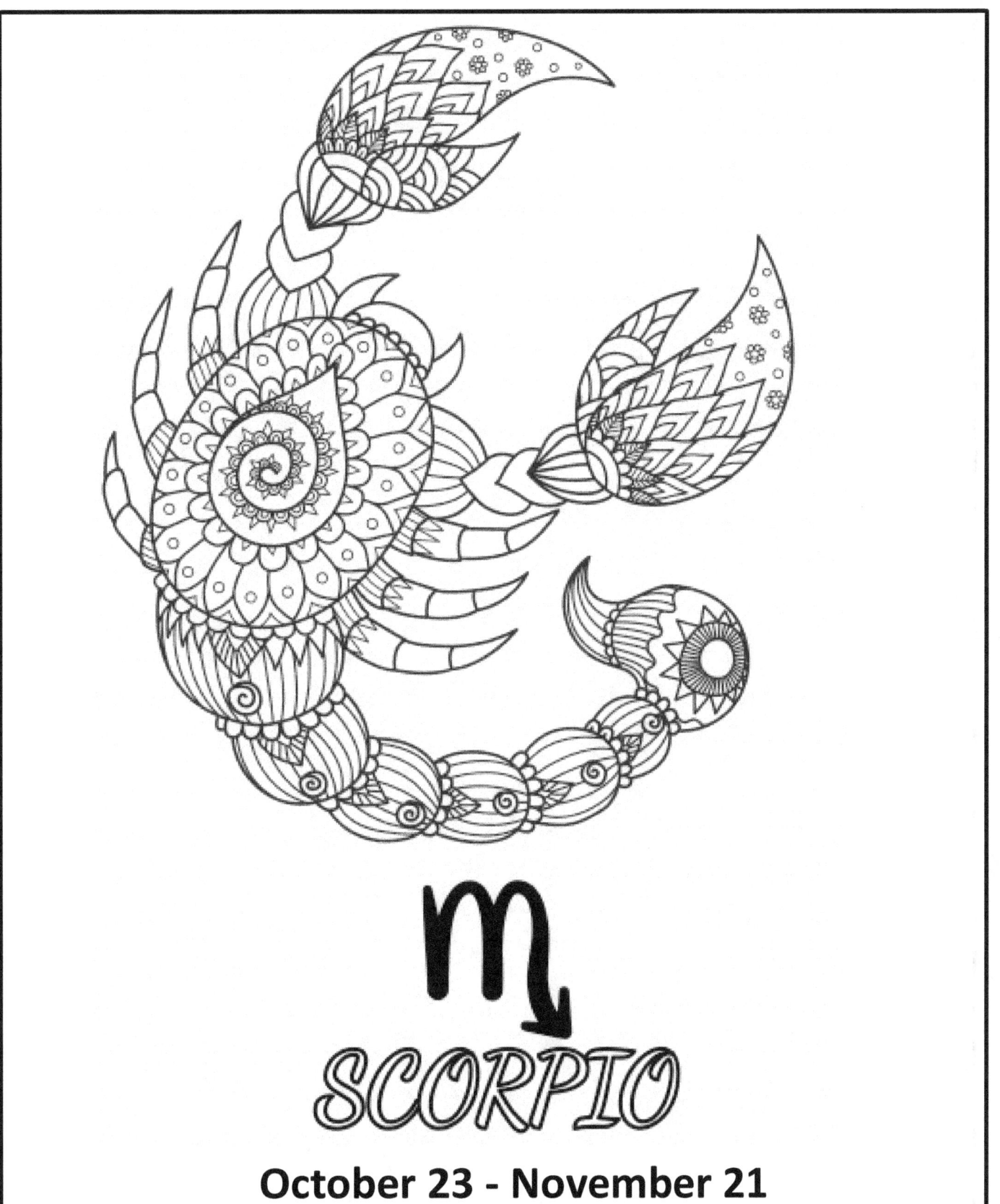

SCORPIO

October 23 - November 21

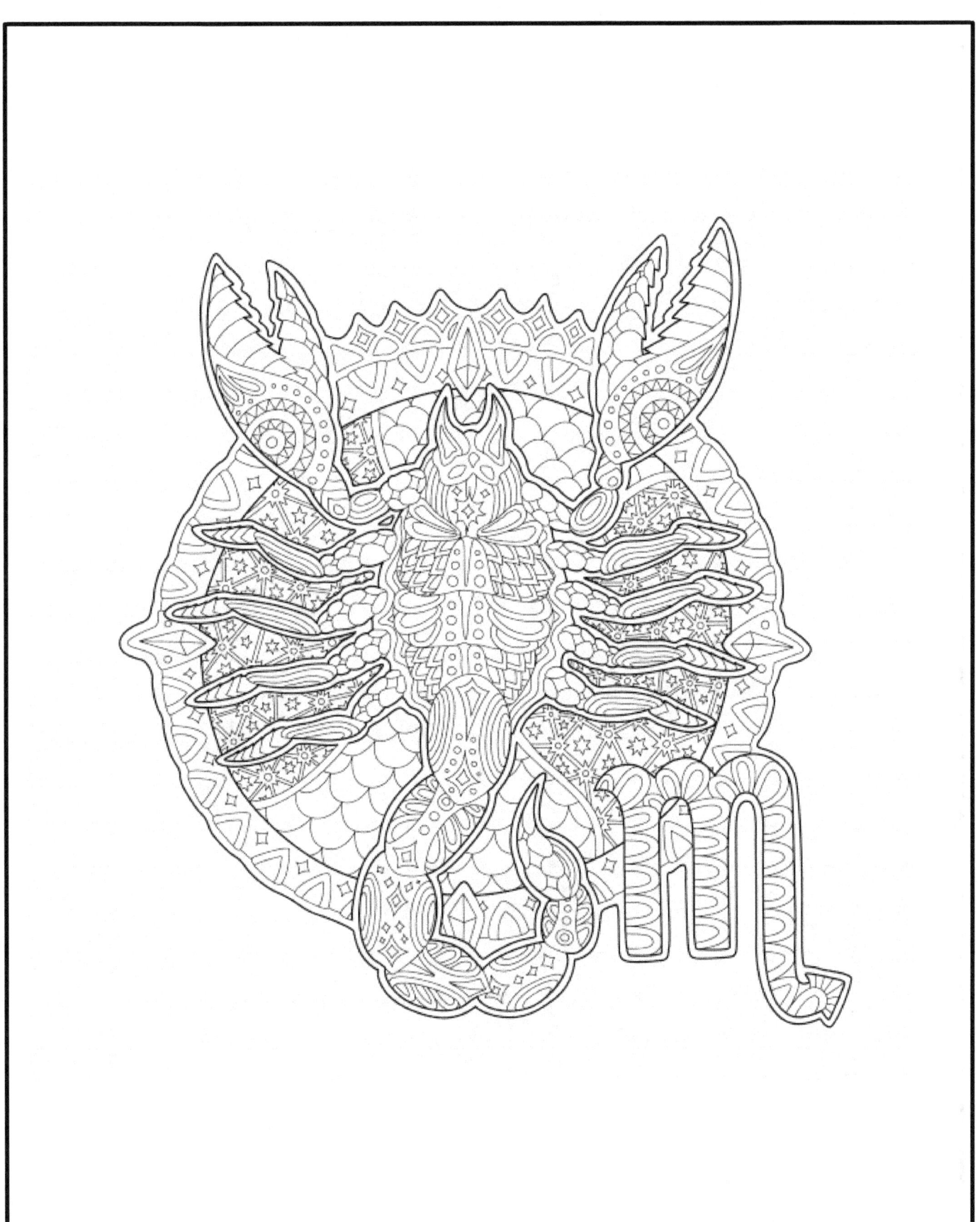

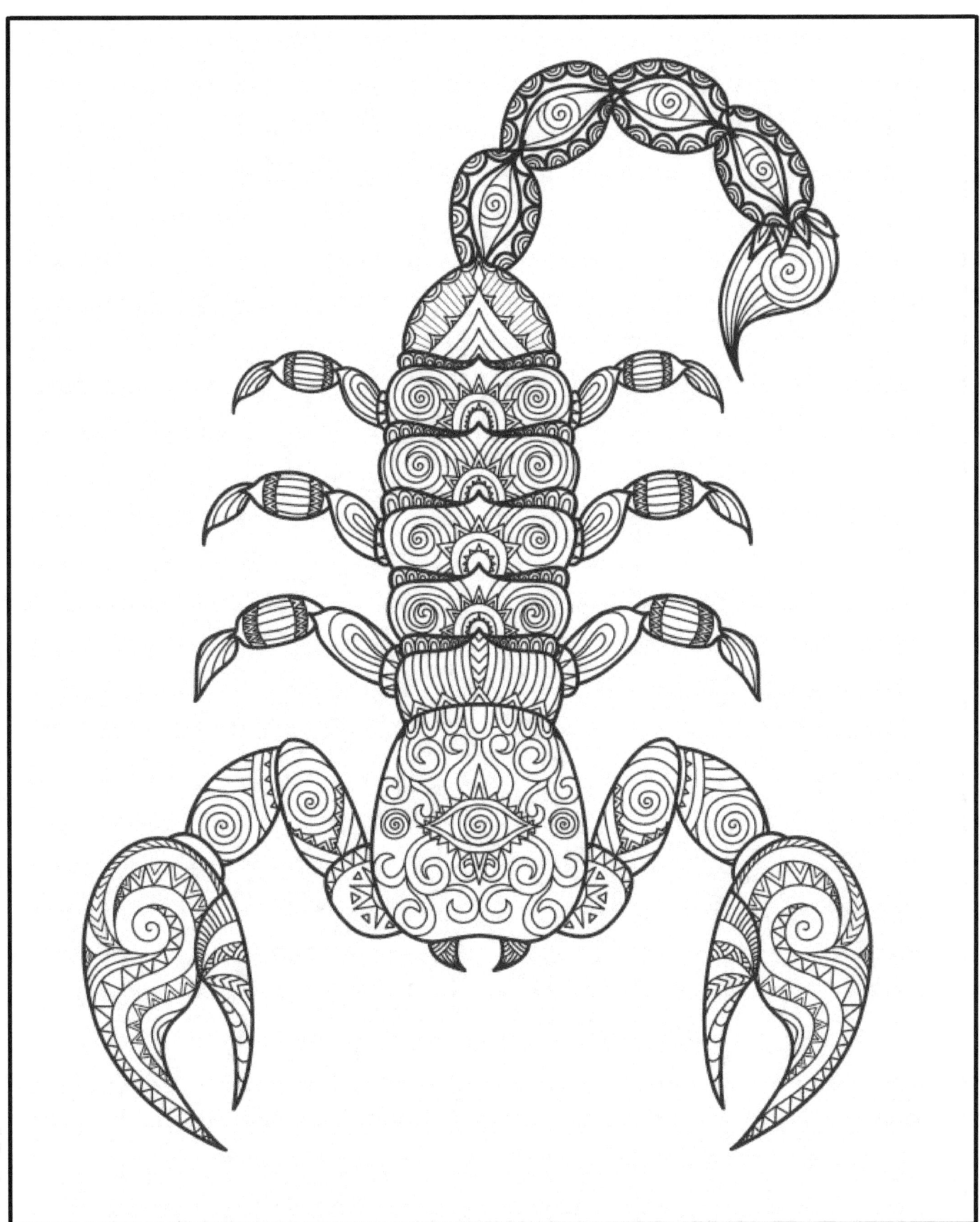

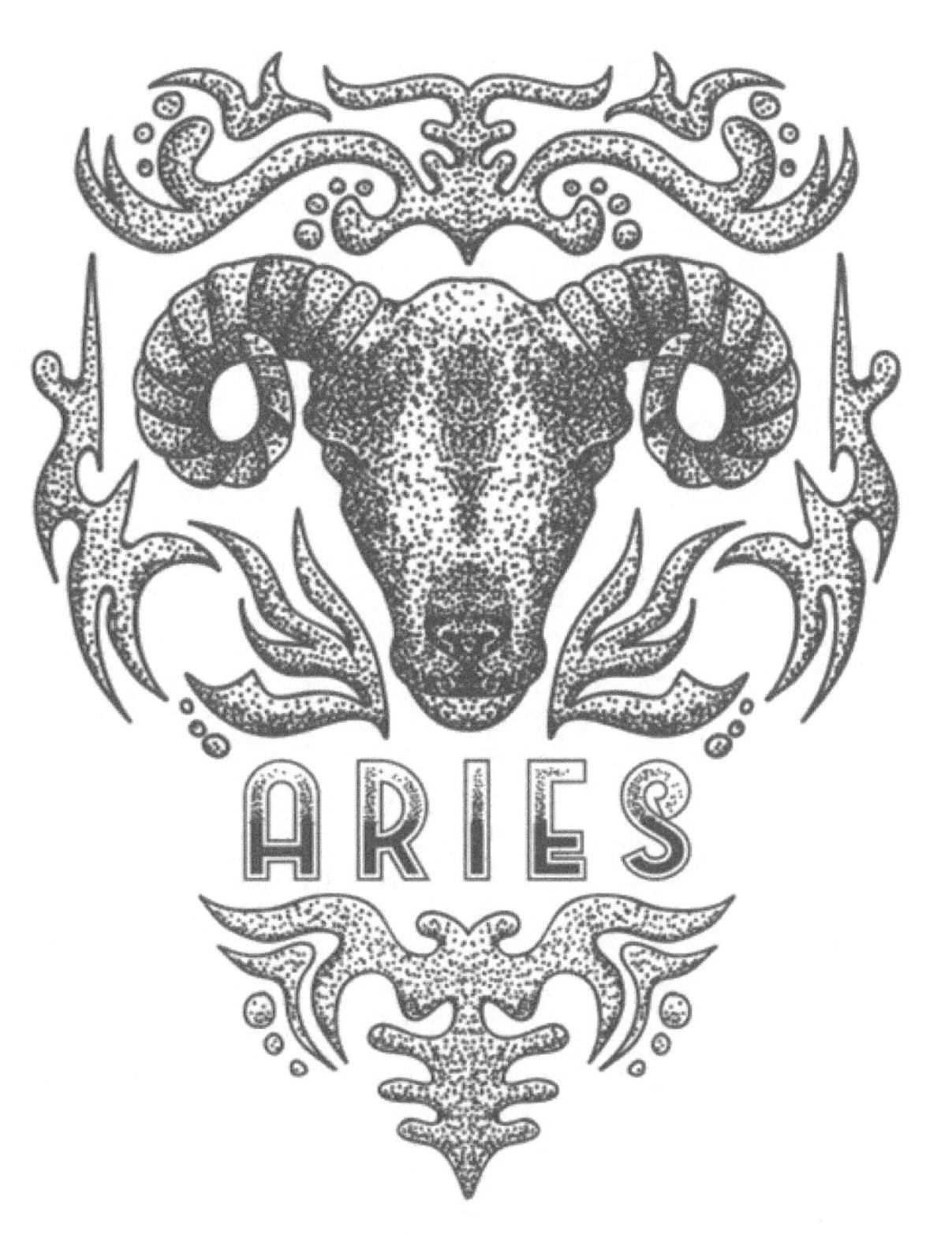

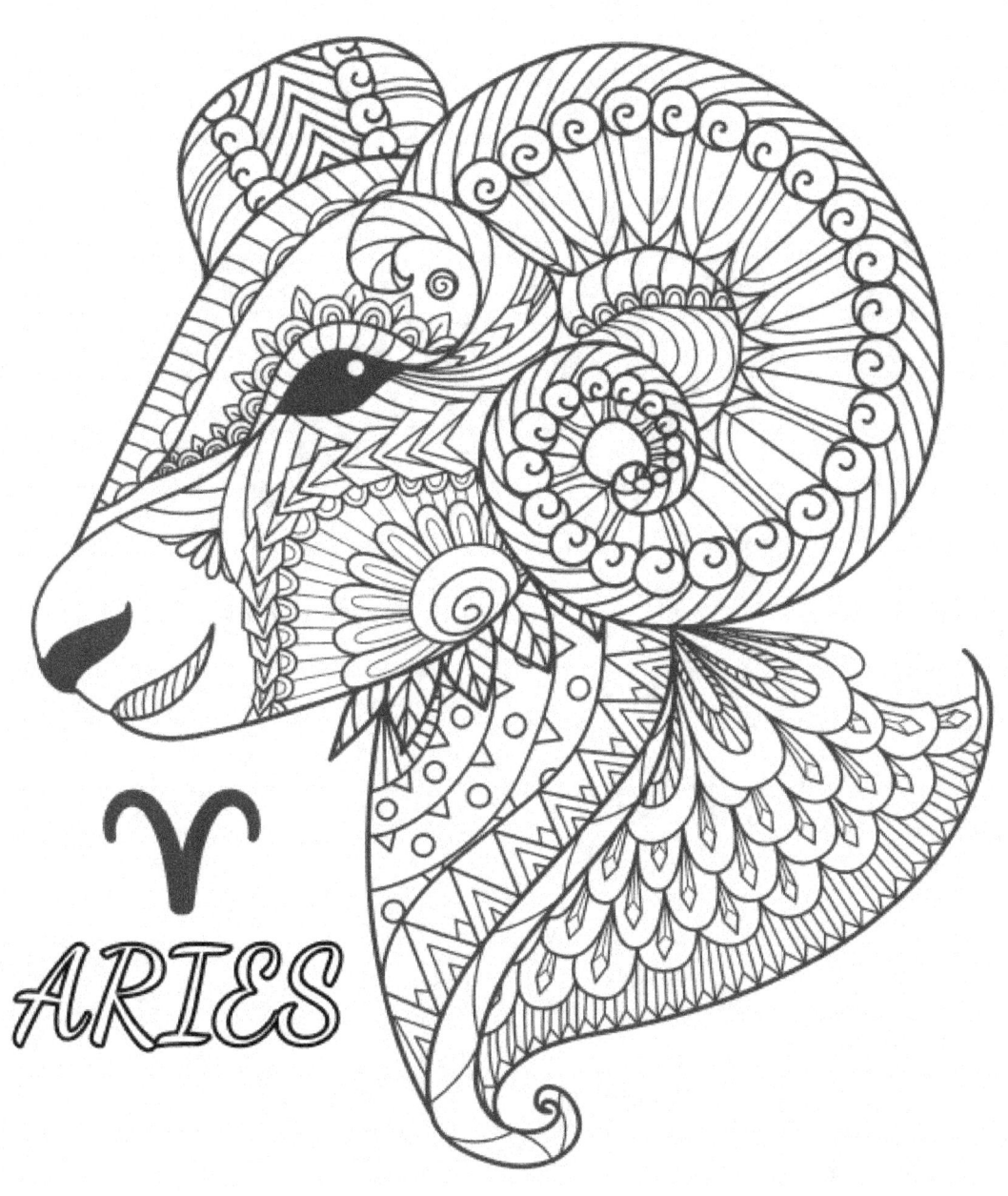

ARIES

March 21 - April 19

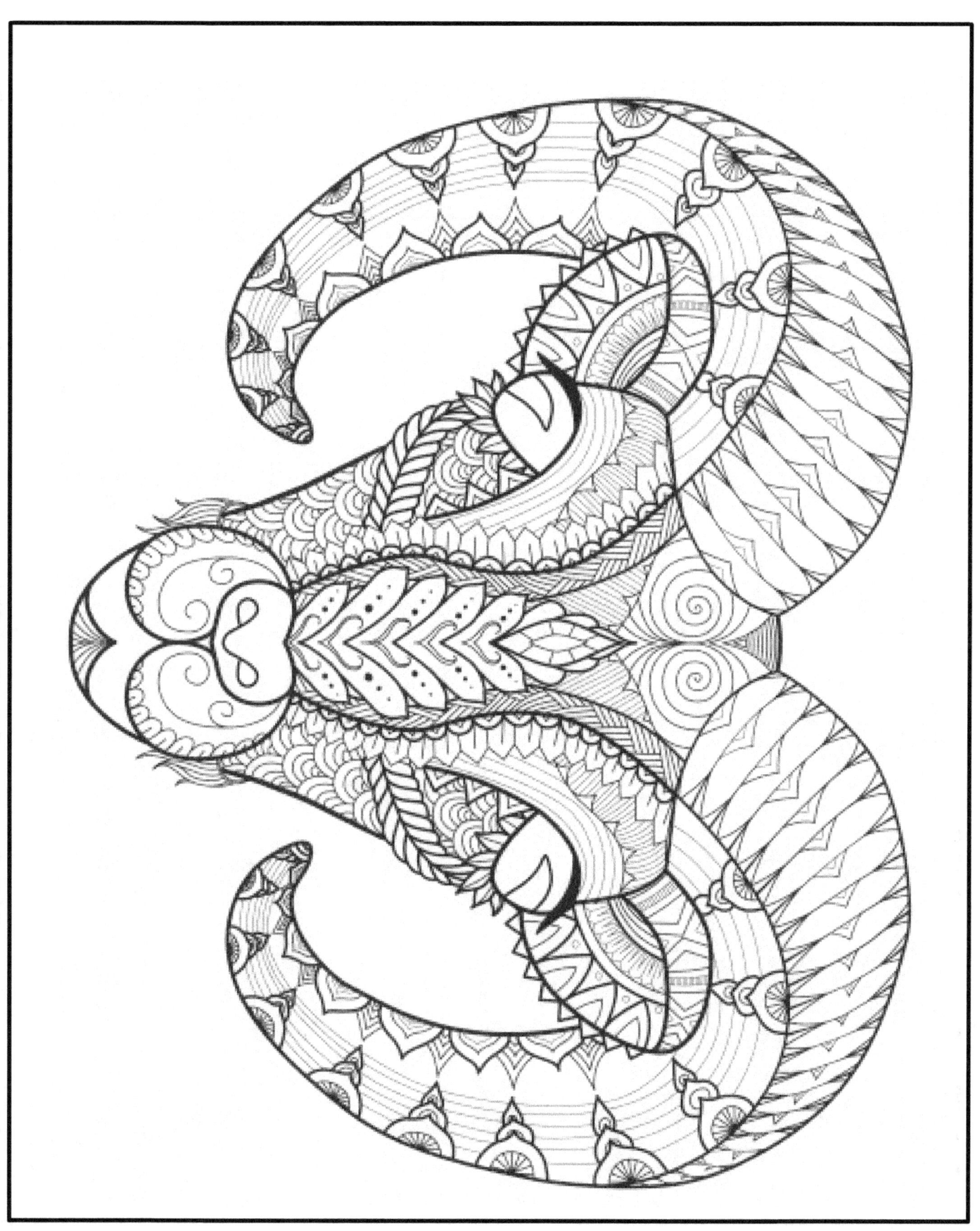

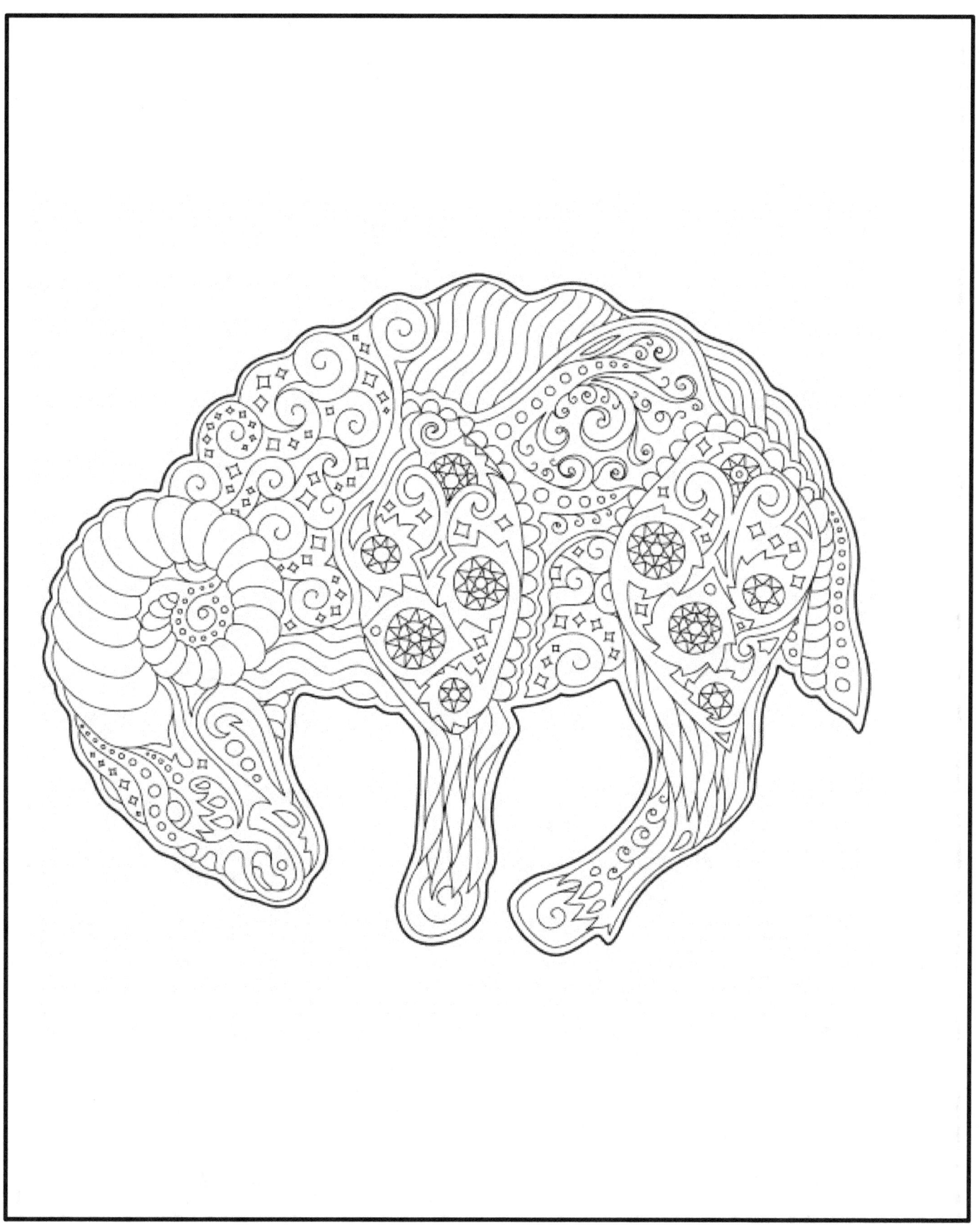

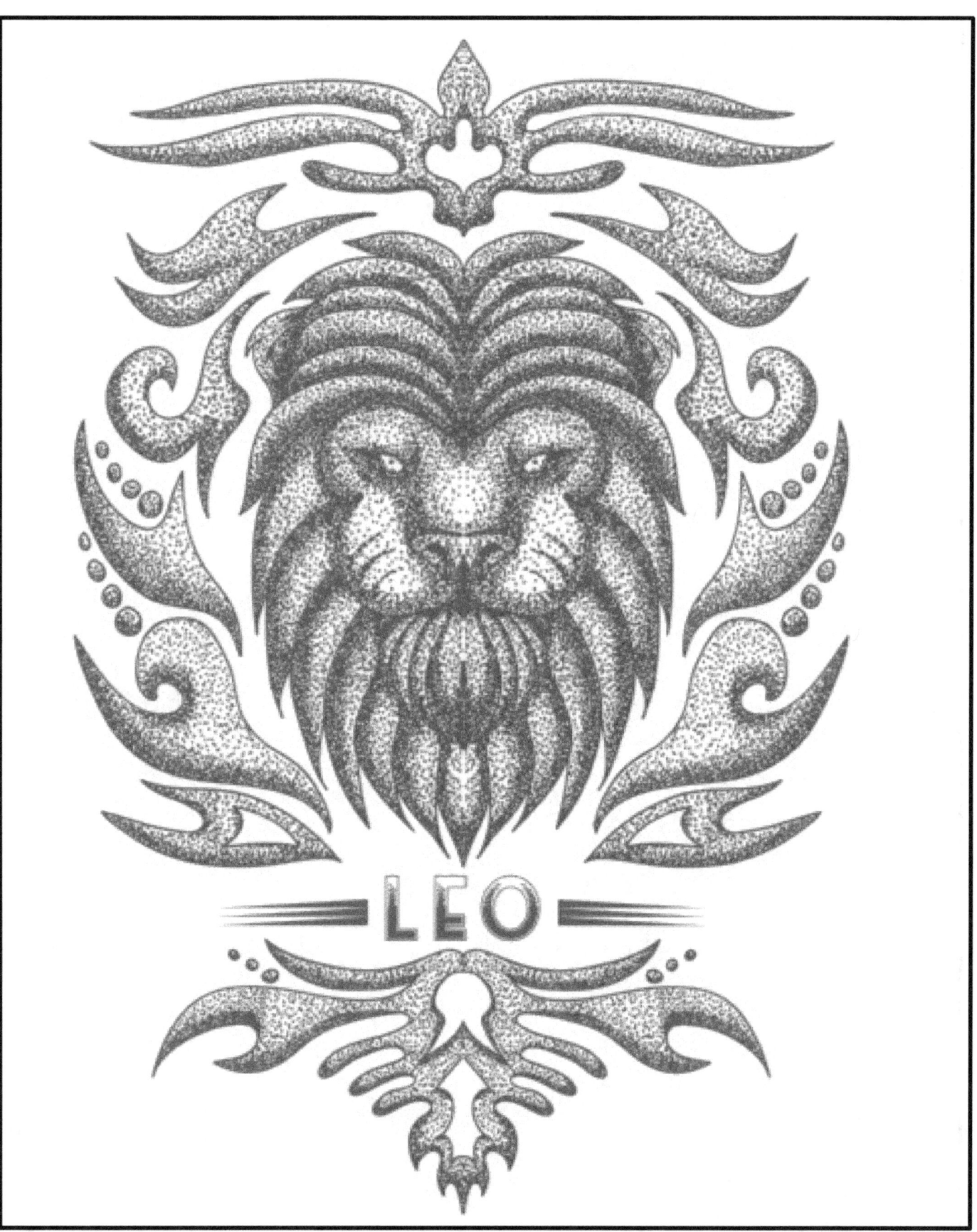